Coronation of an Angel 1st appeared in *Veil*, 2004

Acknowledgments

Cover art by Diane Bombshelter
www.dianebombshelterart.com

Cover graphics and photography by Roman Hansford

Special Thanks to Tina L. Johnson

Forgotten Race
Saving Grace

Poetry by
Tina Huerta

For Rick

Who upon introduction recited poetry to me, who kept a ten-year promise of return, and promised to always hold me before any tear would fall. The angels tell me he is fondly regarded amongst them.

Contents

ASTEROID HYALOSIS

Tiny colored ribbons
softly crushed silk
floating before my eyes.

I've left them everywhere -
in my pockets
in my notebook

on the kitchen table

Waiting to be stretched
Wanting to be long and useful.
Some want to be present bows
Some want to lace my shoes

Others want to decorate the floor.

if you listen to my words
you too might see my tiny ribbons

bouncing in the air.

RIDERS

Stationed thirty-three degrees north
Still hearing echoes
Valleys with higher colder mountains
the sound of hooves
and broken ground beneath
Reminders of missions past
deeds well done
earning placement for this lifetime.

History speaks of coming events
mapped precisely four dimensionally
Players positioned
Ready to Role

THE LANDING

The dirt crumbles off the wall
clutching its precious lint
suspended in captive lullness

a solid landing
bending far at the knees
not intending
so far a bend
- entrophic gravity
Sweat smothering memory
possible direction.
They tunneled through the planet
feeling cool terra
sifting fingers of cold clammy core.

My thick uneven layered crusty garb swaying
loosely camouflaged armor
visioness light nestled securely
within my mind
resting just beneath my skin
blessing my permeating
swishing sound

LABYRINTH

We traveled in lines
mostly frightened
listening for direction
leaders and scouts
spewing and pointing in different directions
bits and pieces of forecasts
Some could see
2 sections down
I could see stories beyond

We traveled in groups
traversing underground bridges
timing our jumps thru pendulum swinging walls
desperate for any way thru
we could see the Minotaurs
reaching down
grabbing hold
and biting off heads

Halfway thru
our group found our underground cliff house
We were given instruments
I was to play the violin blues

Broken instruments to be sure
mishandled by the thousands
only 4 strings and
my bow was only 4 inches short
strung with splitting twine
no hair to be bound
Rob played an old rusty tin.

Brave women came and sang
These were no ordinary
sacrificial lambs
dressed in pleated flowing
chiffon reposed in pale green
arms outstretched to each Minotaur
voices heralding harmonics
formidable phantasmic frequencies
we plucked along

BERTH

out of place architecturally
the sign has a Chinese name
the caretaker has been
                   negligent with the door
we sneak in.
3 of us.
each room has someone sleeping.
Neglected, peaceful, not sanitary
but looked after and left in peace.
all mental patients
the bathrooms are a mess.
we empty Olivia's diapers
and tell her she needs to wear her
                   underpants.

the hallways are small with sharp corners
fabric hangs everywhere.
We wake one of the Residents
He informs us that they each
                    have a special mental gift –
                    and it drains them
one room has twin males
the caretaker finds us talking
                    and asks that we leave.

MESA

You had two rooms
We fled before grampa saw us
there was a party in your day room
we joined – warmed

There are rooms
specific rooms in my dreams

so clear
am I living two lives at once
always other rooms I've lived in
in other parts of the world
places we've rested
eaten
stored food
prepared for show time
walking down corridors
are these generic historical dreams
is there another part of me
sharing with me
trying to communicate with me.

Where are you now?

Why are my dreams so alive
                    I've crossed a line

It's safer than I thought

        I can't paint them
            So I dream of them more
        hundreds of dreams since childhood
                bubbling like parts of a soup
        always waiting for me
                        In the back of my mind

You in the sleeping quarters
        of the Chinese house
                What a mess of fabric
                        in those rooms

All of us in those dreams are conscious
of each other
        do others dream this way?

I believe I've found something
         other than dreaming
a world of places, experiences
   I can enter consciously If I choose.

the question was asked amongst a group
"What do you see in your dreams?"
         Some dreamed in black and white
             Some in symbols
                 Some with no sound

while I dream in full Technicolor.

Forgotten Race Saving Grace, tina

PASSION

the audience gasp gestalt.
        the floorboard
         'neath you
         creaks.

stepping into the future
witness to your demise
your self proclaimed denial
unconscious of the role
 casting the anti-hero
molding yourself
        beyond method
  a banner for their mortal quest

but this is your chosen battle

  warping yourself
      i mark the future scar

lifeline to your soul
        whispering thunder

forgotten tongue
                - forgotten race

a hero's race   most humane.
stage left   grace floats

a milky satin

pause enough
            for breadth

hoping you'll recognize
the sign
  for praise.

BEFORE

When i was 2 you were 2
When i was 2 you were 15
i was born
before you were born

When I was 4
You whispered in the wind
i called to you
i call to you now
you still do not hear exactly
i call quieter with each step forward
waiting for you to step within me
willingly.

WAITING

I Found you out in the trailer house
Resting in the loft.
Your bag was packed
Not ready to leave

I had rushed out of work
they had wanted workers to punch out
I said "put me on salary"

The day was changing the light
You looked exhausted
how long could we stay
waiting for you to go.
You and I waiting

SPIRE

up in a tower
surrounded by clouds

billowiness upon which to ride
firm and soft
upon which to lay at ease

I've known these walls
far too long
gathering, searching, waiting

trinkets of tableau
traverse the table
discovered
in deep jungle
undergrowth

quarried thru
icy blindness
atop this watery sphere

dredged from deep dark
sea graves

rescued as fiery meteors
whizzing by
releasing incantations

captions clearly marked
clues uncovered
bits of puzzle
locking and unlocking

creating serenity of will
in which to grace
anticipated sequestration

strewn fabrics
gathered and mended
by nimble minds
tales and thread

nourishment
swift and sweet
ladled and poured
for our fare

treasured artifacts
culled for wisdom
crafted for lore
kept for our safekeeping.

Forgotten Race Saving Grace, tína

MUSE VARIATION

I am struck
In an unending moment
Reminded by soft undercurrents
of this one moment
The ballroom sways
The crystal syncopating
the dancers' quiver
Of each relieved breath
Layering in step
by tiny step

After all this time
When I heard you again
Biding an introduction
Your words filling my memory
Your voice coming off my chest
Lifting and choraling me forward forever
To this honored motion within your embrace

How could it not be?
I had wondered dismissing its ring
Submerging its significance

Now seated before you
Carefully measuring words
Frightful of your flight
And not your fight
Ages wait upon each approach
I dare speak a small sentence
In response to your steel test
Will you hear the screaming in my head?
"I love you!"

I had a crazy wonderful dream
Last night
The one about the army of guitarist
Sign-language performers
Martial artists
And creatures of unknown planets
I hadn't told you the creatures
Live in water

And so all the performers,
Musicians, Physical Linguists
And Creative Contortionists
Gathered around water's edge
Moving, sliding to a rhythm
Lulling the filter to its might
The spark of origin
Inspiring song from long ago.

I hear that resonance
And feel its orbital pull
Effervescent harmonics
Of what we represent
A mere notion is what is presented
Garbed in swaying of skirts
And firmness of feet
Lifting above the dancing floor.

The muse exists
I cannot in plain conscious dismiss her
The call is gathering
The time is reproaching
Listen quietly, sequestered
In between each note
In between each half-step
In between each heart thump thump.

NYC

Watching out for needles
only fall brown leaves crackle

My soles have blackened
not even a stare

The city doesn't roar
it whispers

ghosts have freedom
Maybe the throng are the ghosts

I only know my skin hairs
against light wind

created by a purposely slow gait

Did I reincarnate as a horse?

No, no my body bounces
two dimensionally

from window to window
fully exposed

never minding
conventions or repercussions

pacing time for acceptance
pacing time for this one moment

covered only in a shroud of thought.

CONFISCATED

I climbed the hill down the street
looking for the gate entrance to the housing complex.

it was just a little wooden gate.
when I went through

a couple of people suggested a couple of parties.
I left about 3am.

I was trying to remain unnoticed. shadowing
myself.

someone else was coming out the gate
behind me

so I slid down the dirt hill
into a soft ditch.

a large group, all decked out, came out.
one of the women found me

covered me with a soft red velvet cape.
the other women protecting me, surrounding my
ditch.

she was well respected.

then a shootout began,
people were running to another building
down the street.

it was the police.

I ran out of the ditch past the police
into the new building.

they had their lights on me

as I slid down cement stairs 3 times.

they were impressed.   I was just doing.

the police left

and I went to another street to another party
                        it was the gypsy house.

        there were people sitting on the floor
in one big room.

                    drugs of all sparkly types
            were being passed around.

two women suggested I try the small metallic
                    brightly colored confetti looking
                        one.

                        I saw what it did to the woman
who was on my left

after she passed it to me
        I saw what this particular drug's effect was.

it was a sex drug.

men who'd taken it
were waiting on the floor,
close to sleep.

then the police came again.
everybody ran out into the street.

we all ended up
at some sort of outdoor
musical gathering

SAMURAI TEST

A longer blade would be preferable,
one with less distance
between thought and hesitation,
course contemplation.

Give me one good reason why not.
What is left? A fucked-up situation.
Lies given. Veil of a dishonest player.

How do I admit that I could be so wrong
Stupidity and naivety
don't come close to betrayal.
So what is left?
A display of self-mutilation
so finely and courageously executed?

I hear shots
bearing different owners in separate situations.
mercuric poisonous desires
trapped within these mountains
This dark moon not her usual self.

My arms have become locked,
ready.
Held in precipitous release.
as has my mind.
In my heart
lay the strength to hold both back.
It is my only hope.
Enough of a realization.
                    Enough for a release

Now I face the other way.
God decided
to make it a two-part essay finals exam.
My muscles need balance.
The moon full has many children,
including unhollistically high machismo border sludge.

Apparently the blade is long enough
to prevent destruction,
at least a bloody mauling.
Body Shock
solid force
against store front window.

The blade still holds the ground.
And that white bitch belly is looking sweeter.
Why not? It's a fucked-up situation.
Why not take the other path?
Why not die another way?
A display of self-mutilation
so finely and courageously executed.

My mate witnesses the temptation
withheld
and slight quiver
over and under
over and under
over and over.

He is positioned for the possibility,
He faces a separate similar battle
discording another direction.

God sent only one frantic pissed-off policeman.
All eight backed off.

CORONATION OF AN ANGEL

Passing through darkened hallowed halls
     past silent restful rooms
The world outside
     awaits in timid hushness.

Pains of his self-hatred
     sweep the separate voids
Cries of his terror
     crack these breathing walls
I solemnly march down forgotten halls
     guided by his grieving.

Mystics left a note on the door
               -"Loving Child"
     etched in crystalline music
Left hand sweats
     turns the knob
The other quivers
     resting against my antique scabbard.

The shifting floor sops in soup
	of vomit, blood and cold sweat
a single candle
	shines overhead.

He lays naked, full-grown
	shivering and scared
on a stainless steel table.
Turning his head
	with those empty begging eyes
He screams -
		Do you love me?
I reach for my dagger
	and whisper in his face-
		Enough to cut
			those scary monsters out.

SUNNY

Angels made special wings
to hold such a gift

Sunny held respect
For Each person
Each creature
In the center of her heart
allowing beauty
to fuse and heal
Each soul.

Angels built special
Pathways for those
who needed to hear
gentle comforts of angels.

We were bestowed
those prayers
Reassurance of a universe
listening realized
delivered by the grail
known as Sunny.

Angels ponied-up
special favors
birthing shimmering offspring
to carry on
Sunny's smile, warmth
and understanding
of the universe's
unfolding breath
inspiring more angels.

SYLPH

The moss is thick, the air cool
   This place of quiet, ancient tranquility
and magical gifts.

            You flutter by
      Silk for wings and golden aura
Emanates from you
                  to all that you behold

      I enter your sphere
Time and place unfold

         The chaos of the world
         Presses every cell
         We sail feverishly
         Reworking, remolding
           Recreating.

            Beauty replacing wailing
      Hope replacing terror
            Desperately racing
   Weaving a future
            For our salvation.

XII HANGED MAN

You're crazy
    if you think
I'm not going to scream, kick, push
      rushing madly into the Universe
Existentially bound.

Let others hold back, stand ashore,
    die slowly.
Every moment I will take
      a song of myself, for myself
Come, fly yourself
Shed darkness, self-deception,
      incriminations

The idea of control
freedom begets freedom
      even if you wish to drown
      within your mind.

To Rainer

KINDRED SPIRIT

Can't even call ya
to sing the crying blues
not cause of you
just save that for some other time

All the words ring so right
"just gotta be a limit"
strings ringin inside my chest
lost somewhere inside my head

can't even call ya
to sing the blues
thumpin and jumpin thru that steel guitar

Riding that never ending train
and that smoke-filled warm summer night

Maybe it's just that magic
of that old steel guitar
hitting that string
you know
each and every one

humpin and thumpin
thru that old steel guitar

Who's gonna sing it
now that you're gone?
Maybe we'll just moan and creak
til we get it something like
strung out in time blues.

CITADEL

Shroud in radiant sunlight we speak solemnly
All the colors of each shiny ornament
pushing thru incandescent white stained glass

Atop the mountain we chase the singing spinning
prayer wheel
We run the halls, laughing, spiritful, breathless
Girls with bangs offering rainbowed beads
Smiling, watching the multicolored mirrored spinning
wheel

Falling silently except for the chorus of the wheels in
my mind
Water hugs each pore
A clean smooth bottomed staircase awaits each
footfall
Slowly, purposefully I search caressing each surface
dimple
I swirl in warm ghostly light

My heart ascends to the top
Deep easy breath
Water floats each follicle
Sun shines my face.

MARTIAN LEGACY

lofting in the citadel
a cloud dust avalanche
mountain experience
EVACUATE THE POPULACE
guide wire harnesses
Strong stretchy straps
You could feel the weight.

sliding down the mountaintop
speeding silky sooty sky
There were no more straps
find a safe place
passed a great church
- not our faith

a warmly lit abide
rooms of awe
- Not unlike Buckingham Palace
clouds burst spilling ash
rooms all filled high
Our room stayed lit
Not all would last thru
We took a deep breath.

THE IMPORTANCE OF CAT EXERCISING

We take for granted
the errands of life
the gas in the car, groceries in the basket
the folds of the towels in the linen closet

The alarm clock sings off the cell
I used to behave so boldly
My older kitty heading towards an early grave
the younger developing self-entertaining neuroses

Time to start the day
scheduling my life away
meetings, networking, shaking hands
organizing, planning and shuffling the future

I watched for weeks
Your dedication to playing with the cats
An hour in the morning
An hour each evening
patiently we – you, me and the cats
We waited, eyes darting, allowing the experience
allowing for your gift to us
to enter into our psyches

After a couple of months
Shadow's vomit production is down
Ticket no longer feels the need
to prove her keep just because she's mostly blind

In watching you I have learned
I no longer feel the volcanic pressure
To squeeze every moment building my projects
feathering my future unjustly
with well trained nimbleness
Instead allowing what is distinctly inside to ferment
with round firmness of a bees dance
No longer feeling the need to overprove myself
just because I'm broken
That life has dealt some awful cruel tinctures

Yes I had survived remarkably
I had the invisible scars to hypnotize me
into catatonic realms of lost time
and spiritual-mutilation
unrecognizing me from those
who might rush in to help
Those who loved me or might just love me
because I had condemned myself
to perpetual self-torture
blaming myself for my innocence
The child abused by my kindergarten teacher.

NONE COMPARE

She swims into my head
rolling her vowels
  letting them roll around
  from deep within
"Don't you know
  you're my surrogate mother?"
The one i miss talking with
Someone who appreciates
being read Shakespeare's Sonnets
absurdities of a purple palace
screaming G*d-crazed neighbors
ridiculous innocence of a 5 year
        old's made-up amusements.

She's hidden herself from me
not because of me
            just recluse
            it hurts
I miss the conversation
  our laughter at the silly world
        and our sigh at the universe

How do you thank someone
  who's left the room?

Wouldn't it be nice
     if it had meant as much to her
Oh guess what Sharon?
I thought it.
I thought about
  what it may have meant
     to you
It meant a great deal to you
     as well.

But silly us —
  if I thought it
  and you meant it
  did anyone hear it?
  And would it make them laugh
in and out for a couple of days?

Would they remember
    to bring out the teacup?
that particular tinkle
 of that teacup with its saucer?

Who else would have the wisdom
    to knock me a "hello"
"Tina – he's gorgeous!"
He was scrumptious too.

You asked me twice
    "But how do you know
G*d really exists?"

G*d exists in every moment
    every movement we make
    every word spoken
    every kiss
    every angry word
    every thought given

Take each step
    with this in mind
      and you will feel the answer
        shift thru time.
  Just try it Sharon –
    give it a whirl
    sprinkle it with
  "Do you think G*d heard that one?"
  Answer yes.
  "Did G*d get the joke?"
  Answer yes.
  "And would it make G*d laugh?"
  Answer yes.
    Maybe even Blessed.

VOICE OF MY WEEPING
-Psalms

If i sit
in the right place
at the right time

The machine loosens
the role collapses
i find my ghost
    that which i've always been

Why i choose this madness
outside the ghost

        she whispers
        sweet caresses of fragile beauty
        within the creases of the machine

    searching, shining

The human artist
      strokes of gesture
      she knows   i know
not until the curtain falls
      last card played

      she waits and knows
forethought unannounced
the tears of prayer
softly goes
      stays throughout
the art of blessing